Exotic Nigerian R

An Illustrated Cookbook of West African Dish Ideas!

BY: Allie Allen

COOK & ENJOY

Copyright 2021 Allie Allen

Copyright Notes

This book is written as an informational tool. While the author has taken every precaution to ensure the accuracy of the information provided therein, the reader is warned that they assume all risk when following the content. The author will not be held responsible for any damages that may occur as a result of the readers' actions.

The author does not give permission to reproduce this book in any form, including but not limited to: print, social media posts, electronic copies or photocopies, unless permission is expressly given in writing.

Table of Contents

Introduction

How spicy are most Nigerian dishes?

Can you alter the spices so everyone will enjoy the experience?

Are suitable substitutes available for typical Nigerian ingredients?

Nigerian food is quite spicy and hot, and it offers a lot of flavors. It uses dry pepper, which is similar in taste to cayenne pepper, and bouillon cubes called "Maggi cubes" for extra flavor. It also utilizes hot peppers, curry and ground crayfish in its recipes.

You can tone down the heat in Nigerian dishes by lowering the amount of cayenne pepper and hot and spicy peppers like habaneros if you're preparing meals for people who don't enjoy spicy food.

What are some everyday dishes in Nigeria that you may enjoy recreating at home?

Nigerians enjoy cereals, sausage, eggs, bread, plantains, bean cakes and bean pudding in the morning. For lunch and dinner, they often prepare dishes with beans, plantains, pasta, yams and rice. Meat and fish are also utilized in Nigerian cooking.

Most of the ingredients used in Nigeria are also consumed in other countries of West Africa. Many of the dishes are made with tomatoes, peppers, spinach and palm or olive oil. Keep reading, and let's cook Nigerian-style!

Nigerian Breakfast Recipes...

1 – Egg Moi Moi

This moi moi breakfast dish is made with eggs for a base, rather than beans. It's a delicious morning meal, easily prepared.

Makes 2 servings

Cooking + Prep Time: 35 minutes

Ingredients:

- Baby spinach, as desired
- 3 eggs, large
- 1 small onion, red
- 1 tin of sardines
- 1 tbsp. of diced peppers, sweet
- Salt, kosher, as desired

Instructions:

Divide ingredients in 2 individual bowls.

Break the eggs and beat them. Salt as desired and mix into eggs.

Slice onions. Distribute them in bowls.

Add beaten eggs, leaves of spinach, sardines and peppers.

Add water to a pot. Place base in pot, forming set-up for steaming. Set on stove and bring to boil.

Place bowls of moi moi in base. Cover bowls with foil. Cover pot. Steam for 8-10 minutes, till moi moi form cakes. Serve promptly.

2 – Nigerian Egg Breakfast Stew

This tasty stew is a popular choice for breakfast in Nigeria. It's delightful to eat and quick to prepare.

Makes 5 servings

Cooking + Prep Time: 20 minutes

Ingredients:

- 8 beaten eggs, large
- 1/2 cup of water, filtered
- 3 tbsp. of tomato paste, no salt added
- 1 pepper, scotch bonnet or habanero
- 1 cup of oil, cooking
- 1/2 chopped bell pepper, green
- 1/2 chopped bell pepper, red
- 1 chopped onion, large
- Bouillon cube or salt, kosher, as desired
- 1/2 tbsp. of garlic, crushed
- To garnish: 1 spring onion stalk

Instructions:

Heat oil in medium pan. Add garlic and onions. Sauté till the onions have softened.

Add tomato paste to pan. Fry for three minutes and stir, so it won't burn.

Add chopped peppers. Cook on low for 2 minutes more.

Add 1 cup of water to beaten eggs. Stir gradually into bubbly stew. Break up eggs by continuously stirring. Serve.

3 – Nigerian Pancakes

These pancakes are supple, delicious and moist. They are not the typical bread-like dry pancakes served in western countries.

Makes various # of pancakes

Cooking + Prep Time: 50 minutes

Ingredients:

- 3 & 1/2 cups of flour, all-purpose
- 1/2 cup of milk, evaporated
- 1/3 cup of sugar, granulated
- 3 eggs, large
- 1/2 tsp. of salt, kosher
- 4 & 1/4 cups of water, filtered
- To fry: oil, vegetable

Instructions:

Break eggs into large bowl. Beat well. Add 1/3 of your water. Stir till combined well.

Sift flour into same bowl. Stir from the middle till mixture is well-combined. Crush lumps, if you see any.

Add evaporated milk, salt and sugar.

Add a little more filtered water. Mix well. Then, add additional water, a little at a time, till you have used up all the water.

Pour a bit of the oil in frying pan. Heat it up. Add thin pancake batter layer.

On medium heat, fry till top of pancake is browned lightly. Flip and fry other side. Repeat with remainder of pancake mix. Serve with your choice of toppings.

4 – Nigerian Yam and "Egg"

This breakfast dish is a much-loved staple in many households of Nigeria. It's easy to make, and it fills you up for the morning ahead.

Makes 2-4 servings

Cooking + Prep Time: 55 minutes

Ingredients:

- 1 peeled, thick-sliced yam
- 1 pack of tofu, regular – silken tofu doesn't work as well here
- 1/2 tsp. of turmeric, ground
- 1 to 2 tbsp. of oil, sunflower
- 1/2 finely chopped onion, red
- 1/2 chopped pepper, red
- 1 or 2 chopped tomatoes, large
- 1/2 finely chopped pepper, scotch bonnet
- 1 stock cube, vegetable
- Salt, kosher & pepper, ground, as desired

Instructions:

Add water and salt to pan. Then, bring to boil. Add yam pieces. Don't over-boil them.

Crumble tofu on cookie sheet. Sprinkle with ground turmeric. Place in oven for 18 to 20 minutes, till most liquid is evaporated.

Heat oil in frying pan. Add stock cube and chopped vegetables. Cook till veggies are just a bit tender.

Remove tofu from oven. Crumble more, as desired. Add to frying pan. Combine all the ingredients well. Season as desired.

When yam has finished cooking, drain off any liquid remaining. Serve.

5 – Potato Omelet

The original Spanish Tortilla de Patatas is the inspiration for this potato breakfast omelet. It's been subtly changed in Nigeria, making it easier to prepare without losing any taste.

Makes 4 servings

Cooking + Prep Time: 25 minutes

Ingredients:

- 3 tbsp. of oil, canola
- 1 ring-sliced onion, medium
- 1 tsp. of minced garlic
- 1 tsp. of pepper, ground
- 1 tsp. of salt, kosher
- 1 tsp. of chili flakes, red
- 7 ounces of tomato, chopped
- 4 ounces of sardines
- 7 ounces of baked beans
- 6 beaten eggs, large
- 4 tbsp. of cubed butter, unsalted
- 5 pounds of potatoes, boiled

Instructions:

Heat oil in non-stick, medium pan on med. heat.

Add garlic, onions, kosher salt, ground pepper & chili flakes. Cook for 1 to 2 minutes. Don't allow the onions to brown.

Add sardines, baked beans and tomatoes. Cook for 4 to 5 minutes more, till liquid is reduced a little.

Stir in eggs. Cook for 2 to 3 minutes. Remove pan from heat.

Place 1/2 cube of unsalted butter on 3 or 4 boiled potatoes. Spoon egg mixture over the top. Serve.

Nigerian Recipes for Lunch, Dinner, Side Dishes and Appetizers...

6 – Clay Pot Chicken

This chicken recipe is made in a Dutch oven, but you can use your earthenware pot if you have one. Either way, the taste is wonderful.

Makes 4-6 servings

Cooking + Prep Time: 2 hours & 25 minutes

Ingredients:

- 1 chicken, whole – pat dry
- Pepper, black, as desired
- 10 tbsp. of butter, unsalted
- 1 & 1/2 tsp. of salt, kosher
- 2 lb. of seasonal vegetables, mixed, like carrots, sweet potatoes, etc. – cut them in 2" pcs.
- 6 scallions, large – cut them in 3" pcs.
- 2 bruised, 3"-cut lemongrass stalks
- 1 crosswise-halved head of garlic
- 1 x 2" piece of ginger, fresh – cut in 1/8" rounds
- 2 lime leaves, fresh
- 10 sprigs of thyme
- 1 lime, fresh – cut it crossways in 1/8" rounds

Instructions:

Preheat the oven to 375F. Insert fingers and loosen skin from drumsticks and chicken breast. Rub 6 tbsp. of butter under the skin. Rub 2 tbsp. of butter in chicken cavity.

Season cavity and outside of the chicken using kosher salt. Use kitchen twine to secure the legs. Lift tips of wings up & over the back and tuck them under the chicken.

In Dutch oven or large pot, arrange veggies, lemongrass, scallions, ginger, garlic, thyme, lime leaves & slices. Lay chicken atop veggies. Cover. Roast in 375F oven for 35-40 minutes.

Remove the pot from oven. Increase temperature of oven to 400F. Wait till it gets to 400F, then uncover pot and return to oven. Roast in 400F oven for 45-60 minutes, till chicken becomes tender and internal temperature is 165F.

Remove pot from oven again, and transfer the chicken to cutting board. Then, allow to rest for 15 minutes or longer. Remove, then discard lemongrass, ginger, thyme sprigs and lime leaves. Squeeze the roasted garlic from skins. Return it to vegetables. Toss pan drippings with veggies and last 2 tbsp. of butter. Carve the chicken. Serve with veggies.

7 – Obe Ata Stew

This is a bright and lively tomato-based stew that includes bell peppers and habanero chilies. The particular recipe also includes sweet potatoes and chicken for a hearty meal.

Makes 4-6 servings

Cooking + Prep Time: 1 & 3/4 hours

Ingredients:

- 1/4 cup of oil, olive or canola
- 4 drumstick & thigh chicken legs
- Salt, kosher, as desired
- 2 de-seeded, de-ribbed, chopped bell peppers, red
- 1 chopped onion, large
- 2 de-seeded, chopped tomatoes, beefsteak
- 2 de-stemmed, de-seeded, halved chilies, habanero
- 1 tsp. of pepper, ground
- 2 cups of chicken broth, low sodium
- 2 1" cubed potatoes, medium
- 1 small spinach bunch with trimmed stems
- To serve: sliced chives, cooked rice

Instructions:

Heat the oil in large pot on med-high. Season chicken as desired. Cook with skin side facing down for 8 to 10 minutes, till skin is crisp and browned. Turn chicken over. Cook till other side is just lightly browned. Chicken will not yet be done. Remove to plate.

Cook the onions and bell peppers in the same pot while frequently stirring for six to eight minutes, till veggies have softened and onions are golden brown.

Add the chilies, tomatoes & pepper. Stir frequently while cooking for six more minutes or so, till tomatoes are softened and broken down. Transfer to food processor. Puree till smooth.

Return the puree to same pot. Add potatoes and chicken. Bring to simmer on med-high. Cover pot partially and lower heat, maintaining the simmer. Cook for 45 to 50 minutes, till potatoes and chicken are quite tender. Chicken will be done cooking, so there should be no pink inside.

Season as desired. Add spinach and stir. Stir while cooking for a minute more, till spinach wilts.

Add stew to bowls. Then spoon rice in bowls, along with chives and chicken. Serve.

8 – Nigerian Vegetable Gbegiri

This gbegiri is creamy and rich. It's a warm and comforting dish that people love.

Makes 6 servings

Cooking + Prep Time: 40 minutes

Ingredients:

- 1 cup of peeled beans, brown
- Pepper, cayenne
- 1/4 cup of oil, palm
- 2 tbsp. of crayfish, ground
- 2 stock cubes, beef
- Salt, kosher, as desired
- 3 cups of beef chunks

Instructions:

Boil the beans with sufficient water on med. heat till soft.

Boil meat with onions, kosher salt & stock cubes till tender. Separate meat from stock. Set aside.

Blend the cooked beans in food processor till smooth. Set them aside. Pass through sieve. Discard chaff.

Place pan over med. heat. Add the oil. Heat for two to three minutes.

Stir the pureed beans in oil. Then, add water as needed for the consistency you desire.

Add meat & cayenne pepper. Combine well. Reduce heat & allow to cook for 8-10 minutes. Check to ensure it doesn't burn. Add additional water as needed.

Add stock cube, crayfish & salt. Cook for three more minutes. Serve.

9 – Afang Soup

This is a soup made with Okazi leaves and spinach. It is loaded with seasonings, spices and protein-laden chunks of vegetables.

Makes 4-6 servings

Cooking + Prep Time: 1 hour & 25 minutes

Ingredients:

- 1 to 2 lb. of meat tripe, cow skin
- 1/2 chopped onion, medium
- 2 tbsp. of bouillon
- 1/2 lb. of fish, smoked, bones removed
- 1/2 cup of crayfish
- 1 to 2 cups of oil, red
- 5 cups of Okazi leaves – you can substitute leaves of spinach
- 6 cups of spinach leaves (in addition to 5 cups of above)
- Salt, kosher, as desired
- Pepper, black, as desired

Instructions:

Soak dried leaves for 10+ minutes. Wash them and drain water off.

In medium pan, boil the meat. Season as desired and add bouillon & onions. Cook onions till tender. Reserve stock.

Boil tripe and cow skin together till tender. Drain water. Chunk-cut the fish.

In large-sized pot, combine meats and fish with one to 2 cups of stock. Cook for three to five minutes.

Pulse Okazi leaves in food processor. Add water.

Repeat step 5 with fresh, chopped spinach.

Stir in oil, crayfish and bouillon. Cover pot. Allow to simmer for a few minutes. Add Okazi leaves to pot and stir. Do the same with spinach.

Combine all ingredients together. Allow to simmer for 15-20 minutes or so. Season as desired. Serve while warm.

10 – Nigerian Peppered Beef Tongue

Peppered beef is dairy free and gluten free. This tasty recipe offers high-quality protein, too. Any meat can be used in it, and the recipe uses beef tongue.

Makes 6-8 servings

Cooking + Prep Time: 1 hour & 50 minutes

Ingredients:

- 3 pounds of beef tongue
- 2 & 1/2 tsp. of chili blend spices
- 2 bell peppers, large, 1 yellow & 1 orange
- 1 plum tomato, fresh
- 1 onion bulb, large + 1/2 bulb for meat boiling
- 3 garlic cloves + 2 more for meat boiling
- 3 chilies, scotch bonnet
- 1 chili, jalapeño
- 1 chili, poblano
- 2 peppers, serrano
- 1/4 cup of oil, olive
- 2 vegetable cubes + 2 more for meat boiling
- 2 tsp. of salt, kosher + extra as needed
- 1/2 tsp. of thyme, dry, +/- as desired
- 1 dash pepper, black
- To garnish: 2 tbsp. of chopped parsley, bell peppers and green onions

Instructions:

Clean beef tongue well. Dry it with layered paper towels. Cut in bite-sized pieces. Add to large pot.

Add 2 garlic cloves, 1/2 onion bulb, 1 tsp. of chili spice blend, 2 vegetable cubes, & 1 tsp. of kosher salt. Cover meat well with water.

Cover pot. Cook till tender. Strain, then set meat aside.

Quarter onions and bell peppers. To food processor, add garlic, onions, tomato & peppers, with the exception of one serrano. Blend roughly, leaving some visible texture.

Set another pan on stove. Add oil. Warm oil up. Add pepper blend to heated oil and stir.

Allow mixture to simmer. Add salt and stir. Add 1 tsp. of chili spice blend and stir. Add vegetable cubes, pepper & thyme and stir well. Taste and adjust seasoning as desired.

Cover pan. Cook over med-low heat till liquid has reduced visibly. This could take 15 to 20 minutes or so.

Stir and season as desired. Add beef tongue and cover with sauce. Cover pan. Simmer over low heat for 5-7 minutes more.

Garnish using serrano, green onions, bell peppers and parsley. Serve with rice or quinoa.

11 – Bean Porridge

This porridge is made in a single pot, so it's easy to prepare. The ingredients are inexpensive and healthy, and the taste is absolutely delightful.

Makes 2-3 servings

Cooking + Prep Time: 25 minutes

Ingredients:

- 2 cups of beans, brown
- 1 red onion, medium
- 2 tbsp. of crayfish, ground
- 2 fresh peppers, scotch bonnet, ground
- 2 seasoning cubes
- Salt, kosher, as desired
- 1/4 cup of oil, palm

Instructions:

Pick through beans and wash them. Rinse and place them in large pot.

Add 1/2 of onions. Add sufficient water to cover veggies well.

Add remaining onions, along with seasoning cubes, pepper and crayfish. Add oil. Season as desired.

Stir the porridge, then lower heat. Cook for 8-10 minutes. Then, remove from heat. Serve.

12 – Nigerian Lamb Stew

This stew is easy to make, especially in Instant Pot. You can always braise it on a stovetop, too, after you prepare it.

Makes 4-6 servings

Cooking + Prep Time: 1 hour

Ingredients:

- 4 tomatoes, fresh or 2 cups of diced tomatoes, canned
- 1 de-seeded, chunk-cut bell pepper, any color
- 1 scotch bonnet pepper, small
- 1 tbsp. of curry powder
- 1 tbsp. of bouillon, chicken
- 3 garlic cloves
- 4 tbsp. of oil, olive
- 1 thinly sliced onion, large
- 2 lb. of lamb, bone-in

Instructions:

Place scotch bonnet, bell pepper, tomatoes, garlic cloves, bouillon and curry powder in food processor. Blend till pureed.

Turn on Instant Pot and set to Sauté. Add oil. Heat for one to two minutes. Add lamb and onions. Cook for 6-7 minutes till onions are turning gold. Add sauce prepared in step 1.

Stir everything well. Turn off Sauté mode. Cover Instant Pot. Set for 20 minutes on High pressure. Allow natural release.

Remove lid. Turn Sauté mode back on. Simmer stew till it has reached your preferred consistency. This takes four to six minutes. Serve.

13 – Pepper Soup

Pepper soup in Nigeria is similar to what the western world calls chicken soup. It's the one that you'll be craving when the weather is bitter cold.

Makes various # of servings

Cooking + Prep Time: 1/2 hour

Ingredients:

- 2 & 1/2 quarts of water, filtered
- 2 & 3/4 lb. of bite-sized cut chicken meat
- 3 tbsp. of pepper soup spice blend, prepared
- 1 bruised lemongrass stalk – cut in three pieces and tie them in bundles
- 1 or 2 bouillon cubes, vegetable
- Red chilies, ground, as desired
- Salt, kosher, as desired
- 2 tsp. of crayfish, ground

Instructions:

Place cut-up pieces of chicken in large-sized pot. Add 2 cups of water. Then add 1 tbsp. of spice blend, bouillon cubes, kosher salt (if desired), red chilies, lemongrass and crayfish. Stir. Let mixture simmer over low heat till liquid starts boiling.

As liquid boils, add remainder of water & remainder of spice blend. Cook over med-low heat. Season as desired. Simmer till the meat has become soft. Serve.

14 – Ewa Riro

This is a delicacy in Nigeria, with a rich flavor that belies the fact that it's simple to prepare. It's an economical dish that makes wonderful stewed beans.

Makes 3-4 servings

Cooking + Prep Time: 1 hour & 40 minutes

Ingredients:

- 3 cups of peas, black-eyed
- 1 bell pepper, red
- 1 onion, medium
- 1 turkey wing, roasted
- 1 pepper, habanero
- 1 tbsp. of crayfish, ground
- 1/2 tbsp. of seasoning blend
- 1/4 cup of oil, palm, +/- as desired
- 6-9 cups of water, filtered
- Salt, kosher, as desired

Instructions:

Pick out any debris from beans. Rinse them and drain well.

Place beans in pot. Add turkey wings, onions, habanero and bell peppers. Add the water. Allow to cook for about an hour, till beans are tender.

Remove onions, bell peppers and habanero. Blend. Add back to beans.

Remove turkey and debone. Cut meat in small-sized pieces. Put back in bean pot.

Add kosher salt, crayfish, oil and seasoning powder. Add water as needed. Stir and combine well.

Allow to simmer for 3-5 minutes. Serve.

15 – Beef Suya

This tasty treat is street food in Nigeria, offering beef that is seasoned with paprika, peanuts, cayenne, garlic, ginger and several zesty spices. It is usually served on skewers.

Makes 6 servings

Cooking + Prep Time: 1 & 1/4 hours + 8 hours marinating time

Ingredients:

- 1 & 1/2 pounds of 1/2"-sliced sirloin steak
- 2 tsp. of salt, kosher
- 1/2 cup of peanuts, dry-roasted, unsalted
- 1 tbsp. of smoked paprika, sweet
- 1 tbsp. of ginger, ground
- 1 tbsp. of garlic powder
- 1 tbsp. of onion powder
- 2 tsp. of sugar, brown
- 1 tsp. of pepper, cayenne
- 1 tsp. of pepper, black
- 1 tsp. of powdered bouillon, chicken
- 1/4 cup of oil, canola
- 1 lemon or lime, juice only, fresh

Instructions:

Pulse the peanuts in food processor till chopped finely. Add onion and garlic powders, ginger, cayenne, kosher salt, granulated sugar, black pepper and chicken bouillon. Pulse, combining well.

Transfer 3/4 of spice mixture made in step 1 to large bowl. Reserve the other 1/4 of mixture.

Add 1/2 oil to bowl from step 2, creating a thick paste. Use your hands to mix well.

Season the beef using kosher salt. Allow to sit for 30 minutes.

Combine the peanut mixture with beef. Toss, coating beef evenly. Cover the bowl. Place in refrigerator for 6 hours minimum. You can leave it overnight, if you like.

Preheat grill for med-high. Brush grate lightly with oil.

Thread the beef onto the skewers. Grill on med-high and turn a couple times, for three to five minutes, till almost cooked through and charred lightly.

Transfer beef to platter. Squeeze with lime or lemon juice. Garnish with last 1/4 of spice blend, as desired. Serve.

16 – Nigerian "Eggplant" Stew

This stew will take you back to your younger days when a bowl of stew warmed you up after being outside in the cold weather. It still works just as well now!

Makes 4 servings

Cooking + Prep Time: 30 minutes

Ingredients:

- 2 eggplants (aubergines)
- 2 tbsp. of oil, olive
- 1/2 cup of onion, chopped
- 2 chopped garlic cloves
- 1 tsp. of paprika, smoked
- 1/2 tsp. of chili flakes, mild or hot, as desired
- 1/2 can of tomatoes, chopped
- 2 flaked, deboned, smoked mackerel fillets
- Salt, kosher, as desired
- 1 tbsp. of parsley, chopped

Instructions:

Remove stem from aubergines. Wash aubergines and cut in small pieces.

Add water to pot. Salt lightly and bring to boil. Cook aubergines for five minutes.

Drain water. Set aside.

Mash aubergines well.

Heat the oil in pan. Add onions. Cook till they are translucent.

Add paprika and garlic. Stir for 1/2 minute.

Add chili flakes and tomatoes. Add 1/2 cup of water from cooking aubergines. Cover pan. Allow to simmer for 8-10 minutes.

Uncover pan. Add smoked mackerel and mashed aubergines. Cook for five minutes. Season as desired. Add parsley and stir. Remove from the heat. Serve.

17 – Egusi Stew

Unlike Nigerian tomato or peanut stews, Egusi stew is not known well by people in the western world. Egusi seeds are not easy to find elsewhere, but you can use pumpkin seeds instead if you need to.

Makes 3-4 servings

Cooking + Prep Time: 55 minutes

Ingredients:

- 1 lb. of smoked meat – beef & turkey
- 1/2 chopped onion, medium
- 2 or 3 chopped tomatoes, medium
- 1/2 cup of oil, cooking
- 3 garlic cloves
- 1/2 tsp. of paprika, smoked
- Pepper, ground, as desired
- 1 cup of egusi or pumpkin seeds, ground
- 1/3 cup of crayfish, ground
- 2 to 3 cups of spinach, frozen or fresh

Instructions:

In medium pot, boil the beef with salt, as desired. Add pepper, onions and paprika and cook till tender. Be sure to add enough water that you end up with 3 to 4 cups of stock for cooking. Remove meat. Reserve stock.

Heat oil in heavy pan on med. heat. Add turkey and crayfish. Continue to cook. Add tomatoes and their juices. Stir well. Add one to 2 cups of the beef stock. Bring to boil. Simmer for five minutes more.

Add egusi or pumpkin seeds. Continue to simmer for about 10 minutes on med. Add additional stock till you reach the consistency you desire.

Add spinach. Allow it to simmer for 4-5 minutes. Season as desired. Serve while warm.

18 – Beans with Corn - Adalu

This is sometimes cooked with fish and sometimes with meats, or both. You can add a stew base of crayfish powder if you like. This is a plain and simple recipe that brings out its unmasked rich flavor.

Makes 6 servings

Cooking + Prep Time: 55 minutes

Ingredients:

- 1 pound of beans
- 1 x 15-ounce can of corn, sweet
- 2 chopped onions, medium
- 1/2 cup of oil, palm
- 1 chopped pepper, habanero
- 1/2 chopped bell pepper, red, medium
- Optional: 1/2 tbsp. of sugar or your favorite sweetener

Instructions:

Wash the beans. Add to a pot of water. Bring to a boil.

Cook the beans for 1/2 hour. Add bouillon and salt, sugar or sweetener, as desired, and 1/2 chopped onions. Cover the pot. Continue cooking and top off the water as needed, till beans are soft and fully cooked.

As beans cook, prepare the base with onions and peppers. Heat oil in saucepan. Sauté other 1/2 of bell pepper, habanero and chopped onions for a few minutes, till all ingredients are tender and soft.

Add corn. Reduce heat level to low. Stir in sauce. Mix well. Add water if beans are dry. Stir again, and turn heat off. Serve while warm.

19 – Fried Plantain - Dodo

Dodo is an excellent recipe to try as the first of your forays into Nigerian cooking. That's because it's quite easy to make. Dodo makes a wonderful side dish for lunch or dinner.

Makes 6 servings

Cooking + Prep Time: 20 minutes

Ingredients:

- 4 plantains, very ripe
- For frying: oil, vegetable

Instructions:

Fill skillet or pan 2" deep with vegetable oil. Heat on med-high for five minutes or so.

Skin plantains and cut into 1" slices. Add to heated oil for frying. You may need to do them in batches, which is fine.

Let slices of plantain cook for five minutes, and then flip them over. You want both sides golden brown. Remove and place plantains on plate lined with paper towels.

Repeat frying with remainder of plantain slices. Serve.

20 – Nigerian Akara

Akara are deep-fried and tasty Nigerian fritters made with black eyed peas or brown beans. They can be served by themselves or with a burger or side dish.

Makes 6-7 servings

Cooking + Prep Time: 5 & 1/2 hours

Ingredients:

- 1 & 1/2 cups of peas, black-eyed
- 1/2 onion, red
- 2 peppers, habanero or scotch bonnet
- 3 tsp. of bouillon, vegetable
- Salt, kosher, as desired
- To deep fry: oil

Instructions:

Soak black eyed peas in water for three minutes and the skin will wrinkle. Place them in a food processor along with water to cover them. Pulse for five to six minutes, separating skin from black eyes peas.

Pour black eyed peas in bowl. Rinse a few times, separating black eyed peas from skins. Drain skins off with water. Soak black eyed peas in clean water for four hours minimum. You can soak them overnight if you prefer.

After black eyed peas are done soaking, drain water and rinse them.

Grind scotch bonnet peppers in food processor till they form rough paste. Set them aside.

Blend black eyed peas with onions and 1/2 cup of water till fully smooth.

Heat oil for your deep frying in pan.

Add kosher salt, scotch bonnet peppers and bouillon to black eyed pea batter. Mix for five minutes or so.

Drop batter one spoonful after another into hot oil. Then, fry for three to five minutes per side till both sides are golden brown. Remove from frying oil. Place on plate lined with paper towels, so they can drain. Serve while hot.

21 – Ogbono Soup

This hearty and tasty Nigerian soup is made with ogbono seeds. You can use pumpkin seeds if ogbono seeds are not available in your area. Pre-cooked meat is added to fill out the flavor – it's delicious!

Makes various # of servings

Cooking + Prep Time: 1 hour & 20 minutes

Ingredients:

- 1 to 2 lb. of meat, your choice of cow skin, tripe, stew beef or oxtail
- 1 cup of fish, smoked
- 1 cup of onion, diced
- 1/2 cup of crayfish, ground
- 1 tbsp. of bouillon, chicken
- 3 cups of chopped kale, collard greens or spinach
- 1/4 to 1/3 cup of oil, palm
- 1 tbsp. of pepper flakes, red
- 1/2 cup of ogbono or pumpkin seeds, ground
- Salt, kosher, as desired
- Pepper, black, as desired

Instructions:

In medium pan, boil the meat, seasoned as desired, for 30 to 60 minutes, till tender. Add the smoked fish. Reserve three to 4 cups of meat stock.

Mix ground ogbono or pumpkin seeds with oil. Add to boiled meat pot, then add scotch bonnet and crayfish. Bring to boil. Then, simmer and allow to cook for 10 minutes minimum. Add bouillon, if desired.

Add additional stock water if needed, till you reach the thickness you desire. Then, add spinach or other greens and cook for another two to three minutes. Turn off heat. Serve hot.

22 – Chin Chin

This is a commonly enjoyed Nigerian snack. It's also eaten in other countries of West Africa. It's crunchy and tasty, considered a delight.

Makes 10 servings

Cooking + Prep Time: 55 minutes

Ingredients:

- 1 & 3/4 cups plus 2 tbsp. of flour, all-purpose
- 1/3 cup of sugar, granulated
- 4 tbsp. of butter, salted
- 1/2 tsp. of nutmeg, ground
- 1 egg, large
- 1/4 cup of milk, evaporated
- 1/2 tsp. of baking powder
- To deep fry: oil, olive

Instructions:

Mix the dry ingredients in bowl. Set bowl aside.

Mix wet ingredients except butter in separate bowl. Set it aside.

Add the butter to dry mixture. Combine with fingers.

Pour in remainder of wet ingredients. Mix together till it forms a dough.

Wrap the dough in cling wrap. Allow to set on kitchen counter for five minutes or so.

Unwrap the dough. Roll it out into 1/4" thickness. Cut dough into small squares.

Place small squares in bowl. Sprinkle them with flour and shake it around so they won't be sticky.

Heat oil. Fry dough pieces till light gold in color. Remove and lay out on layered paper towels. They will start out soft, but as they cook, they will harden. Serve.

23 – Pounded Yams

In this recipe, the yams are stirred or crushed into a creamy consistency, rather like dough. They are a starchy type of side dish, often served with stew.

Makes various # of servings

Cooking + Prep Time: 35 minutes

Ingredients:

- 2 to 3 lb. of yams, Ghana or African

Instructions:

Peel yams using sharp knife. Don't remove too much flesh.

Remove spoiled spots, discolored areas or bruised areas as you're peeling.

Cut yams in large chunks. Immediately wash so they don't become discolored. Allow them to sit in cool water till you're ready to use them.

Add yam chunks to med. pot with sufficient water to cover them. Season as desired.

Boil yams till tender, then remove from the heat. Drain in colander. Reserve some yam cooking water.

Pour pounded yams in food processor. Begin to blend, then change to pulsing every 20 to 30 seconds, checking for smoothness. Add water as needed till you have the texture you desire.

Wrap in parchment paper or cling wrap. Serve.

24 – Nigerian Red Stew

Tomato lovers enjoy this tasty stew. It is blended well, then cooked and fried till it naturally sweetens and darkens.

Makes 4-6 servings

Cooking + Prep Time: 1 hour & 50 minutes

Ingredients:

For stew:

- 1/4 to 1/2 cup of oil, vegetable
- 3 lb. of chunk-cut chicken
- 4 chopped tomatoes, Roma
- 1 x 28-ounce can of plum tomatoes, whole, peeled, liquid discarded
- 2 tbsp. of tomato paste, no salt added
- 1 chopped bell pepper, red
- 2 peppers, habanero
- 1 sliced onion, medium
- 1 & 1/2 tsp. of thyme, dried
- 1 tbsp. of red pepper, Nigerian if available
- 1 tsp. of flavor seasoning, like Accent®
- 1 bay leaf, medium
- 1 bouillon cube, chicken
- Salt, kosher, as desired
- Pepper, ground, as desired
- 1 cup of stock, chicken
- Water, filtered, as needed

For chicken

- Salt, kosher & pepper, ground, as desired
- 1 tbsp. of thyme, ground
- 1 tsp. of powdered garlic
- 1 bouillon cube, chicken

Instructions:

Preheat oven to 350F.

Wash chicken. Cut in bite-size cubes.

Place chicken pieces in pot. Add filtered water, bouillon & thyme. Season as desired. Cook chicken till done. Fry till golden brown in color.

Place chicken on rack. Cook in 350F oven for 8-10 minutes and set aside.

Blend tomatoes with bell and habanero peppers in food processor till pureed.

In large-sized pot, heat oil. Add sliced onions and fry just till they have turned golden brown.

Add tomato mixture. Fry for 25 minutes, till mixture has reduced. It should turn a deep shade of red, and oil will start separating from tomatoes. Continuously stir so that mixture won't burn. Add tomato paste. Fry for another five minutes.

Add stock and seasonings. Stir together. Add extra water as needed. Continue simmering for 12-15 minutes. Serve with beans or rice.

25 – Jollof Rice

This is a dish commonly prepared in Nigeria and some other countries of Africa. The recipes differ from one nation to the next, and this is the delicious Nigerian version.

Makes various # of servings

Cooking + Prep Time: 1 hour & 20 minutes

Ingredients:

- 5 chopped Roma tomatoes, medium
- 1 chopped bell pepper, red
- 1 chopped onion, medium – set it aside
- 2 peppers, habanero
- 1/4 cup of oil, groundnut (peanut)
- 3 tbsp. of tomato paste – no salt added
- 2 cups of rice, parboiled
- 2 & 1/2 cups of stock, chicken
- 1 tsp. of salt, kosher, as desired
- 1/2 tsp. of thyme, ground
- 1 tsp. of seasoning, all-purpose
- 1 stock cube
- 1/2 tsp. of curry powder
- 3 bay leaves, medium
- Water, filtered, as needed

Instructions:

Combine tomatoes and peppers in food processor for 45-50 seconds and blend well.

In medium pot, heat oil over med-high. Once oil is hot, add set-aside onions. Fry till they have turned golden brown. Add tomato paste, then fry for two to three minutes.

Add blended tomato and pepper mixture except for 1/4 cup – set that aside. Fry mixture with tomato paste and onions for 1/2 hour or so. Stir as needed, so you don't burn tomato mixture.

After 1/2 hour, reduce heat level to med. Add stock. Mix well. Add seasonings. Boil for 8-10 minutes.

Add parboiled rice to pot. Mix well with stew. Add bay leaves and cover pot. Cook over med-low for 15 to 30 minutes.

When liquid is nearly dried, add remainder of tomato stew. Cover pot. Then, allow to cook for 5-10 more minutes till liquid completely dries up. Turn off heat. Mix well. Serve.

Nigerian Dessert Recipes...

26 – Waina

This rice dish is made in the shape of mini cakes and uses short-grained rice. It's the preferred rice in the Northern regions of Nigeria.

Makes 2 servings

Cooking + Prep Time: 50 minutes + 6-8 hours sitting time

Ingredients:

- 2 cups of rice, short grain – you can use jasmine rice if you like
- 1 tbsp. of yeast
- 1 tbsp. of sugar, granulated
- 1 tbsp. of oil, vegetable
- 1/2 tsp. of ginger, grated

Instructions:

Soak 1 cup of rice in filtered water. Add 1/2 tbsp. of yeast. Allow to set for 6 to 8 hours.

Boil other rice cup. Mash it well, then set it aside.

Pour soaked rice in food processor. Add mashed rice. Blend till rice is smooth.

Into blended mixture, add sugar and ginger. Add last tbsp. of yeast. Allow to rise for 1/2 hour or so.

Grease a pan lightly. Add mixture. Brown on one side. Then, flip and brown second side. Serve with your favorite syrup.

27 – Banana & Coconut Loaf

This is a favorite cool-weather treat, but you can make it in warmer weather, too. You'll probably love every bite of it, as my family does.

Makes 12 servings

Cooking + Prep Time: 55 minutes

Ingredients:

- 1 & 1/4 cups of plain flour, sifted
- Optional: 2/3 cup of coconut, unsweetened
- For topping: small-sized handful of coconut, unsweetened
- 1 cup of brown sugar, light or dark
- Optional: 1/4 cup of oats or nuts, your choice
- 1/4 cup of raisins
- 1/2 cup of room-temperature butter, unsalted
- 2 room-temperature eggs, large
- 1 tsp. of vanilla, pure
- 1 tsp. of salt, kosher
- 1 tsp. of baking powder
- 1 tsp. of baking soda
- 3 bananas, over-ripe
- 1/2 orange – juice and 1 tsp. of zest only

Instructions:

Preheat oven to 350F.

Mash bananas. Set them aside.

Mix wet ingredients. Set them aside, too.

Mix dry ingredients, except for butter and sugar. Set bowl aside.

Mix sugar into butter till creamy. Mix that with wet ingredients. Add bananas and mix again.

Fold dry ingredient mixture into bowl used in step 5. Don't overmix them.

Pour mixture into oiled, flour-dusted loaf pan. Spread coconut onto dough. Then, bake in 350F oven for 45 to 50 minutes. A toothpick inserted in middle should come back clean. Serve.

28 – Nigerian Puff Puff

This is a recipe for a homemade dessert that is popular street food in Nigeria and other African countries. It is delicious and very addictive, too.

Makes 4 servings

Cooking + Prep Time: 1 hour & 25 minutes + 1-2 hours rising time

Ingredients:

- 2 cups plus 1-2 tbsp. of warm water, filtered
- 1 x 2 & 1/4 tsp. packet of yeast, active dry
- 3 & 1/2 cups of flour, all-purpose
- 1/2 to 3/4 cup of sugar, granulated
- 1/2 tbsp. of salt, kosher
- To deep-fry: oil, vegetable

Instructions:

Mix the water, yeast, sugar and salt. Set bowl aside for five minutes or so.

Add the flour to same bowl. Combine well. Allow mixture to rise for one to two hours.

Pour oil into medium pot till 3" deep. Place pot over low heat.

Grab a small amount of batter with your hands. Drop in oil. Continue to add dough balls to oil.

Fry dough balls for several minutes, till bottoms are golden brown in color.

Turn balls over. Fry for several minutes till other side is also golden brown.

Remove balls from oil. Then, place on paper towels to absorb excess oil. Roll balls in sugar if you desire. Serve.

29 – Egusi Brittle

This is a straightforward and easy recipe for a delicious dessert. It takes 1/2 hour or less to make, and once you've made it once or twice, you can be creative with your ingredient choices.

Makes 1-2 servings

Cooking + Prep Time: 25 minutes

Ingredients:

- 1/4 cup of melon (egusi) seeds
- 1/4 cup of peanuts, unsalted
- 2 tbsp. of sesame seeds
- 1 tbsp. of oil, coconut
- 1 & 1/2 tbsp. of syrup, maple
- 1 tsp. of vanilla extract, pure
- 1/2 tsp. of salt, kosher
- 1 tsp. of powdered cinnamon
- 1 tbsp. of sugar or honey
- 1/3 cup of Zobo leaves, candied – available online
- 1/4 cup of coconut, desiccated
- 2 & 1/2 tbsp. of chocolate, melted

Instructions:

In medium bowl, mix peanuts, egusi, sesame seeds, cinnamon, honey or sugar, coconut oil, syrup, salt and vanilla.

Grease parchment paper. Use it to line a cookie sheet.

Pour mixture from step 1 on cookie sheet.

Heat oven up to 350 degrees F. Place cookie sheet in and bake for 8-10 minutes.

Reduce heat to 180 degrees F. Bake for 12 minutes more.

Remove pan from oven. Spread melted chocolate gently over mixture. Top with Zobo leaves and coconut. Place in refrigerator and allow mixture to cool. Then break into pieces and serve.

30 – Nigerian Coconut Balls

Also known as Shuku-Shuku, this delicious treat was first made in Nigeria. It is now made in other African countries too, because of its wonderful sweet taste.

Makes 14 balls

Cooking + Prep Time: 40 minutes

Ingredients:

- 1 cup of coconut flakes, unsweetened
- 1/4 cup of sugar, superfine or caster
- 3 yolks from large eggs
- 1/2 cup of flour, self-rising

Instructions:

Preheat oven to 350F.

In medium mixing bowl, combine egg yolks, coconut and sugar, forming stiff dough. Form the dough in 1" balls. Roll balls in flour, coating them.

Place balls on cookie sheet with 2" between them.

Bake in 350F oven for 18-20 minutes, till golden. Serve.

Conclusion

This Nigerian cookbook has shown you…

How to use different ingredients to affect unique African tastes in many dishes.

How can you include Nigerian recipes in your home repertoire?

You can…

Make Nigerian pancakes and egg moi moi, which you may not have heard of before. They are just as mouthwatering tasty as they sound.

Cook soups and stews, which are widely served in colder months in Nigeria. Find ingredients in meat & produce or frozen food sections of your local grocery stores.

Enjoy making delectable seafood dishes of Nigeria, including hake fish and mackerel. Fish is a mainstay in Africa, and there are SO many ways to make it great.

Make dishes using beans and other vegetables in African recipes. There is something about them that makes the dishes more delectable.

Make many types of desserts, including waina and coconut balls, sure to be tempting to everyone's sweet tooth.

Enjoy the recipes with your family and friends!

About the Author

Allie Allen developed her passion for the culinary arts at the tender age of five when she would help her mother cook for their large family of 8. Even back then, her family knew this would be more than a hobby for the young Allie and when she graduated from high school, she applied to cooking school in London. It had always been a dream of the young chef to study with some of Europe's best and she made it happen by attending the Chef Academy of London.

After graduation, Allie decided to bring her skills back to North America and open up her own restaurant. After 10 successful years as head chef and owner, she decided to sell her business and pursue other career avenues. This monumental decision led Allie to her true calling, teaching. She also started to write e-books for her students to study at home for practice. She is now the proud author of several e-books and gives private and semi-private cooking lessons to a range of students at all levels of experience.

Stay tuned for more from this dynamic chef and teacher when she releases more informative e-books on cooking and baking in the near future. Her work is infused with stores and anecdotes you will love!

Author's Afterthoughts

I can't tell you how grateful I am that you decided to read my book. My most heartfelt thanks that you took time out of your life to choose my work and I hope you find benefit within these pages.

There are so many books available today that offer similar content so that makes it even more humbling that you decided to buying mine.

Tell me what you thought! I am eager to hear your opinion and ideas on what you read as are others who are looking for a good book to buy. Leave a review on Amazon.com so others can benefit from your wisdom!

With much thanks,

Allie Allen